GENTLE EXPEDITIONS

Prayer stones, raven, and Ama Dablam. JONATHAN WATERMAN

GENTLE EXPEDITIONS
A Guide To Ethical Mountain Adventure

BOB McCONNELL

THE AAC PRESS
GOLDEN, COLORADO

THE AAC PRESS

Published by
The American Alpine Club
710 Tenth Street
Golden, Colorado 80401

The AAC was founded in 1902 and began publishing in 1907. It is a public foundation supported by concerned alpinists. The Press is dedicated to the dissemination of knowledge pertaining to conservation, safety, and the art of mountaineering.

This publication made possible through the support of W.L. Gore & Associates, manufacturers of Gore-Tex® and WindStopper® fabrics and the Premier Sponsor of AAC Press.

© Bob McConnell 1996
All rights reserved.

ISBN 0-930-410-63-7   Manufactured in the U.S.A.

Cover photo: Looking north, 25,000 feet, Everest. MICHAEL GRABER/MG
Back cover photo: MARK JONES

To *Scott Fischer* from whom I learned so much about the mountains, about people, and about life.

— Bob McConnell, May, 1996

Acknowledgments

I would like to thank my secretary, Gail Deal for the endless hours she spent deciphering my scribbling. Without her efforts, time, energy and assistance this would never have gotten to press. I also would like to thank Dan Gardner, Kitty Calhoun-Grissom, John Hart, Steve Kin, Phil Powers, David, Liz and Peter Nichol, and Jonathan Waterman for commenting on and contributing to the manuscript.

On September 28, 1996, the Board of Directors of the American Alpine Club established the Scott Fischer Memorial Conservation Fund. Grants from the fund will be made to expeditions that are environmentally proactive.

Contents

	INTRODUCTION 11
1	HISTORICAL OVERVIEW 15
2	THE CHALLENGE 31
3	PLANNING 41
4	IN THE FIELD 69
5	POST TRIP 89
6	WHERE DO WE GO FROM HERE? 93
	APPENDICES 101
	REFERENCES AND SUGGESTED READING 112

Introduction

IT'S TIME FOR ACTION

Mountains make up one-fifth of the world's land mass. Many have special spiritual, religious or symbolic significance; all have diverse, fragile ecosystems. Almost 80 percent of the world's fresh water supply originates in mountain watersheds. Mountains are home to one-tenth of the world's population. People in mountain communities are often marginalized, isolated, and lacking political power. Many live in deep-rooted poverty and face problems including political oppression, overpopulation, food shortages, lack of renewable energy sources, loss of traditional culture, and deforestation.

Many will not view the problems addressed in this book as critical. A Tibetan nomad who fears his son will be murdered by Chinese soldiers, or an underpaid Nepalese porter with a large family,

Gentle Expeditions

or a westerner widowed by a death on the mountain — many might not view environmental problems as major. Nor will political leaders in developing countries. People in Brazil think littering is socially progressive as it creates more jobs for street sweepers. Yet the last unspoiled places on earth, many in remote mountain areas, are disappearing one by one. David Brower has said: "There is alot to be learned from climbing mountains, more than you might think, about life, about saving the Earth, and not a little about how to go about both." Our children's children should have the opportunity to enjoy and learn from the mountains: their rugged beauty, their diverse wildlife, their rare ecosystems, their fascinating cultures. We who visit the mountains need to take the initiative and act as responsible guests in the places we visit rather than add to the problems. This book explains how to do that by distinguishing between the ethics and style of mountain travel. These ideas are tested in the Himalayas, yet they have much broader applicability. These methods will enable mountain travelers to become gentle expeditions.

The concept of wilderness ethics is not new. Aldo Leopold wrote of the need for a land ethic in his classic *A Sand County Almanac* in 1949. More recently, Laura and Guy Waterman built on his ideas in their book *Wilderness Ethics*. The concept was extended to climbing in 1993 by Phil Pow-

Introduction

ers in *NOLS, Wilderness Mountaineering*. Ethics define right and wrong. Unethical behavior is unacceptable. A breach of ethics should not go unnoticed or unpunished.

Style, on the other hand, involves choosing an acceptable alternative. One is free to choose styles of behavior. You might not respect another's choice — such as fixing ropes, using bottled oxygen, or using siege tactics on an expedition. You may criticize and attempt to change another's choice. Regardless, a choice of one style over another is acceptable. Unethical behavior is not.

Alpinists are increasingly aware of how fragile the great ranges are and how our adventures can have a lasting negative impact. Stories of trashed-out approaches and photos of tents pitched amid piles of rubbish have caused many to regret the role they played in creating these problems. Yet awareness is not enough; it's time for action. The growing trend to close climbing areas, even entire mountains, highlights the need to address the problem now. We must each adopt a personal commitment to avoid unethical behavior. We must strive to leave as little trace of our passing as possible in the mountains.

The shelves are besieged with books about mountain travels. They detail mountaineers' accomplishments, failures, problems and routes. In effect, Tenzing Norgay — who first reached the

Gentle Expeditions

summit of Mount Everest with Sir Edmund Hillary in May, 1953 — best anticipated the need for this book when he said: "The tourists who come to Nepal to see the wilderness are actually destroying it."

"Take only photos, leave only footprints." "Pack it in, pack it out." "Leave no trace." These are worthy goals. Yet goals alone are not enough. This book is a primer toward proven, practical ways to accomplish those goals. This starts with a recognition that the only way to eliminate all impact is to stay home. Impact can, however, be reduced from unacceptable to acceptable levels. This book is about how to travel in the mountains without destroying them, and leaving them better than we found them. Although written from the viewpoint of planning a climbing expedition to the Himalayas, these methods have universal application for photographers, trekkers, fishermen, mountain bikers, runners and other visitors to mountains around the world.

Historical Overview

1

Mount Everest serves as a good case study of the impact tourism has had on the remote mountains of the world. Tibetans call it Chomolungma, Goddess Mother of the World. It is the highest, most sought-after mountain in the world. It symbolizes physical challenge, spiritual renewal and grand esthetics.

Everest and its surrounding valleys were first explored by western people in a series of British expeditions in the 1920s. When George Leigh Mallory's team crossed the Pang La and descended into the Rongbuk valley in 1921, they walked off the map. Tibetans were living there as they had for centuries. Men wore animal skins, hunted game and herded sheep, goats and yaks. Women wove the woolen clothing they and their children wore. Barley was ground into flour called tsampa. Men, women and children drank copious amounts of tea mixed with butter, salt and tsampa. The people were deeply religious;

Gentle Expeditions

most valleys housed a monastery. Wildlife was abundant. Streams were pure. Litter was non-existent.

Those first explorers wore hobnail boots, tweed coats, "woolies and windproofs." They used what came to be known as siege tactics, hiring Sherpa "tigers" to make repeated carries to stock fixed camps up the mountain. One of the team members, Noel Odell, later reminisced, "Frostbite? I didn't get frostbitten. We were tough in those days." As tough as they were, they also enjoyed creature comforts. They toasted each other with fine champagne and ate the best food they could bring from England. After descending from the North Col in 1922, Mallory wrote his wife that he had eaten four whole quails truffled in *pate de foie gras*, followed by nine sausages, and was still hungry. They also carried the first tanks of bottled oxygen ever used by mountaineers.

Mallory and Andrew Irvine disappeared on their summit attempt in 1924; Irvine's ice axe was found in 1933. Although on each expedition, the teams abandoned tents, oxygen bottles and other gear at the North Col and above, no trace of their passing remains. Everest was able then to hide all signs of man's intrusions.

What these earliest expeditions did leave, however, is the legacy of siege tactics still in use

Historical Overview

today. Today the trend is toward smaller, lighter, alpine-style expeditions, yet many teams attempting Everest continue to use tactics the British pioneered in those earliest expeditions. Large teams today hire scores of porters or yaks, enjoy creature comforts, and establish fixed camps. Many abandon gear just as the British did in the 1920s. As a result, the signs of their passing are everywhere. Everest can no longer heal itself.

Visitors to the Rongbuk and other remote valleys in the Himalayas may still see people living much the same way as Mallory saw them in the 1920s. Men — often dressed in animal skins — still herd yaks, goats, and sheep. Women thresh barley by beating it with long poles. Broken grain is thrown in the air so the chaff will blow away, leaving the edible kernel behind.

The Rongbuk monastery, which had been home to as many as 2,000 monks and nuns when the British first visited, was destroyed during the cultural revolution in the 1970s. Today it is slowly being rebuilt. Wildlife is often seen above it where killing animals is forbidden by Buddhist tradition. It is our good fortune that Everest and the surrounding mountains are just as spectacular today as they were in the 1920s.

Sadly, today's visitors to Everest and many other places also find "the dark side" of adventure travel. While the situation is improving,

Gentle Expeditions

valleys are often strewn with "white man's prayer flags", or toilet paper. Tin cans and cigarette butts mark trails as prolifically as traditional rock cairns. By the mid 1980s, at K2 Basecamp in Pakistan, expeditions sometimes found themselves forced to pitch tents on piles of rubbish left by their predecessors.

What was acceptable to Odell and Mallory in the 1920s and to Hillary and Norgay in 1953 can no longer be justified. This is not to criticize what they did, but merely to recognize that Everest and many other mountains around the world can no longer sustain behavior that was acceptable

Trashed out Camp 4 on Gasherbrum II. CHARLEY MACE

Historical Overview

in the past. We should, at the same time, recognize that today's formulation of acceptable behavior is no more eternal than those of the past. What constitutes acceptable behavior requires constant review as our numbers increase and as technology improves. Hopefully, 70 years from now, readers will note with interest the primitive methods discussed in this book, just as we look back now at the methods used 70 years ago by the great pioneers of climbing in the Himalayas.

WHY DID THIS HAPPEN?

The most important factor contributing to the "dark side" of adventure travel has been the explosive growth in the number of travelers who visit mountain areas. Inexpensive international airfares have resulted in dramatic increases. The construction of airfields in remote valleys has allowed more people to go deeper into the mountains.

Some statistics will help put this in perspective. Two hundred people were given permission to travel in Nepal in 1950, the year Maurice Herzog reached the summit of Annapurna (the first ascent of an 8,000-meter peak). Two hundred and fifty thousand people visited Nepal in 1988. Over 330,000 visited in 1993. Tourism in Bhutan increased from 287 visitors in 1974 to

Gentle Expeditions

almost 4,000 in 1994. An estimated 352,000 foreign tourists visited Pakistan in 1992. Millions visit China and India each year. This not only puts pressure on the environment, but it has changed the way many mountain people live. The infrastructure in many developing countries has not kept pace with the growth in local populations, much less these dramatic increases in the number of foreign visitors.

Many Americans have learned outdoor skills using *The Boy Scout Handbook*. As late as 1966, it advocated cutting pine-boughs and ferns for beds, using branches for tent pegs and saplings for tent poles. Today, if each camper felled trees to make tent pegs, poles and a bed, whole forests might disappear. What made sense when fewer people visited the mountains is no longer acceptable given the number of visitors today. Many such activities are, with good reason, now discouraged if not prohibited.

During Bill Tilman and Charles Houston's southside reconnoiter of Everest in 1950, theirs was the only expedition in the Khumbu Valley. They saw no other westerners. As they walked up the valley, they found thick rhododendron forests bordering the trail on either side. In *The Ascent of Everest*, John Hunt, leader of the 1953 expedition, describes walking through colorful rhododendron and magnolia trees interspersed

Historical Overview

with giant firs, early spring flowers and fragrant flowering shrubs bordered the path. He described Thyangboche as one of the most beautiful places in the world with a foreground of dark firs, lichen-draped birch, and altitude-dwarfed rhododendrons. Tilman and Hunt's teams enjoyed evening camp fires while their porters used wood fires for cooking.

Indeed, Thyangboche is still a beautiful place, yet many of the beautiful forests Hunt described are gone. Had anyone told Tilman or Hunt in the 1950s that they should not burn wood or the forests would disappear, they might have thought the person insane. Yet 40 years later, a blink of the eye in geologic time, the once lush forests in the Khumbu and elsewhere are often found only in isolated protected areas.

Hillary admits that when he went to Everest in 1953, he "heaved rubbish around with the best of them." Today, the Khumbu valley hosts 10,000 visitors a year. Most hire porters or a yak and driver to carry their gear — quickly escalating the number of people from 40,000 to 50,000 a year. Deforestation, rubbish, human waste and toilet paper are the legacy of our adventures in that valley.

It has been estimated that over 700 tons of garbage were left in the Everest Basecamp in 1979 and 1988. These problems, created by an in-

Litter around Rongbuk Monastery. Bob McConnell

creasing number of visitors, are not limited to the highest mountains. Rubbish has been heaped on well worn tennis-shoe trekking routes as well. Trekkers who wouldn't think of throwing a candy wrapper on a trail near home find it too hard to carry their litter past these piles of rubbish. Many succumb to the temptation to add their refuse to the existing piles. Pack it in, pack it out loses much of its meaning when "out" means back to Kathmandu or Rawalpindi — two of the filthiest cities in the world. An attitude of "the locals don't care, why should I" has certainly exacerbated the problem.

Far too many people who travel in the remote mountains of the world today say "but we are pushing the envelope" to justify littering like Mallory in 1924, Herzog in 1950, and Hillary in 1953. Climbers are happy to escape from what Reinhold Messner named the death zone. Their haste to leave has resulted in abandoning gear, rubbish and even the bodies of those who perish in this, all too often, deadly sport. Yet in May, 1993, a mere 40 years after the first ascent, 39 people reached the summit of Everest in one day! A young woman from Darjeeling, Kunga Bhutia, was 18 when she reached the summit that day. She recalls traveling amid 40 climbers who left the South Col just after midnight. The line wound its way up to the Hillary

Gentle Expeditions

Step where a half-hour traffic jam developed.

Kunga reported that oxygen bottles littered not only the South Col and the route above, but the summit itself. Such numbers give serious question to whether "pushing the envelope" is any longer a valid excuse for trashing the highest peak in the world. If numbers alone do not convince one, technology has written a new chap-

Abandoned oxygen bottles, South Col, 1963.   BARRY BISHOP

Historical Overview

ter in mountain travel Helicopters now fly in to camps as high as 20,000 feet to haul the exhausted and injured back to Kathmandu. Calls from the summit of Everest have become commonplace. Staff, often the indomitable Sherpa people, carry gear, bring hot tea before one rises from a down sleeping bag, and lead climbers to the summit.

Commercial operators offer guided climbs of Everest for $65,000. Anyone with enough money can make a summit attempt, with high-altitude porters to carry their oxygen bottles and only one

The South Col, 25 years later. SCOTT FISCHER

Gentle Expeditions

trip in and one trip out of the dangerous Khumbu Icefall. We have come a long way since the British walked off the map wearing woolies and windproofs in 1921, but not too far to apply advancing technology to minimizing our impact in the mountains. Just as visitors to parks in America no longer cut pine branch beds, we should no longer litter trails, camps or even the summits of mountains in other countries.

Popular mountains all over the world are beginning to reach, or have exceeded what bureaucrats call their "carrying capacity." Managers are imposing stiff regulations and higher fees. In some cases, mountains are closed entirely to our adventures. Hillary proposed in the early 1990s that Everest be closed to climbing for five years. Yet he realized the economy of Nepal and many developing countries are far too dependent on tourism dollars for such suggestions to be adopted. We tourists who come to see wilderness seem destined to destroy it by our numbers alone unless we don't change our ways. Because even if numbers are reduced, the problems will continue to mount unless behavior changes.

Fortunately, numbers alone do not make the problem insurmountable. By comparison, 25,000 visitors float through the Grand Canyon on the Colorado River each year. Yet the river remains pristine. It is kept that way by the strict enforce-

Historical Overview

ment of regulations regarding garbage and human waste. "Pack it in, pack it out" has real meaning there. Commercial outfitters who ignore this precept risk losing their permits. Those on private trips are given detailed briefings on acceptable behavior. Peer pressure on the river ensures that the rules are followed. This demonstrates that "carrying capacities" can be maintained or even increased, without harm to the environment, if visitors behave responsibly. The lesson for mountain travelers is obvious. Thousands of people travel down one narrow canyon a year leaving no trace. The mountains of the world deserve the same respect.

PAST EFFORTS TO FIX THE PROBLEM

Before we consider what needs to be done, it is worth reviewing what has been done in the past to reduce the impact of mountain travel. These efforts have, at least in the great ranges, focused on litter. The first thing that comes to mind is the traditional bonfire. Typically, garbage from a trek or expedition has accumulated in a pile. When the group is ready to depart, leftover kerosene is dumped on top and ignited. Everyone feels good about having taken care of their rubbish. Yet these piles almost always contain glass, tin cans and waterlogged cardboard which will never burn. The bonfire is often at high-enough altitude that keep-

Gentle Expeditions

ing any fire burning is a tremendous challenge. Kerosene burns quickly; the rest smolders until the fire goes out, leaving a pile of semi-burned garbage.

What comes to mind next is dumping garbage in a crevasse. Theory has it that a glacier is like a giant garbage grinder. Glaciers are, after all, constantly moving over rocky valley floors.

Burning garbage at K2 Basecamp. CHARLEY MACE

Historical Overview

Whatever goes in, if it ever comes out, will have been ground to dust. The theory may be wrong. A member of the first American Everest expedition was killed in 1963 when a huge serac collapsed in the ice fall. His body was left buried under tons of ice. Barry Bishop who was a member of that expedition, and reached the summit in 1963, was in Nepal in 1972 when he heard reports that a body had been discovered at the foot of the Khumbu glacier. Traveling to the Basecamp, Barry recognized his friend. After nine years, a camera was still around his neck, an ice axe still in his hand.

More recently, a prehistoric man washed out of a glacier on the border between Austria and Italy. Scientists were able to determine what he had for lunch the day he died over 6,000 years ago. So much for the ground to dust theory. All too often, what goes in a crevasse gets frozen in place. It will stay exactly the way it was thrown in unless it falls to the bottom of the glacier where it may be ground up as the glacier moves along the valley floor. Dead batteries and medical waste thrown in a crevasse will, even if ground up, still remain toxic.

Leaving food and gear for the local people is another oft-used technique. This is also problematic. While it may make team members feel good, all too often, local people don't understand the

Gentle Expeditions

value or use of leftovers. Unless time is taken to explain what is being left and how it is used, abandoned items may just be picked over for cigarettes, liquor and candy, leaving the rest to blow away haphazardly.

Even the best efforts to do it right often lead to a frustrating lack of success. The October-November 1993 *Climbing* Magazine carried a story by John Middendorf in which he tells about paying porters in the Baltoro to carry out several hundred pounds of garbage after climbing Great Trango Tower. Their Pakistani liaison officer later ordered the porters to throw the garbage in the Braldu River!

Awareness of these past efforts and respect for their good intentions is important. Yet, as pointed out, each has had its shortcomings. Moreover, the problem goes far beyond litter. It is time to not only improve on past efforts but also address a broader range of issues including erosion, wood depletion and deforestation, toxic wastes, noise and visual pollution and cultural impacts.

The Challenge

2

> *We must learn to discipline ourselves again. Discipline is a virtue that has been lost and forgotten in our society. Self-restraint and patience have also been consciously discarded in the all-out pursuit of freedom and hedonism.*—Rush Limbaugh

Why would anyone quote this man in a book about protecting the mountains? Well, he is right! The great paradox for mountaineers is that many see climbing as an expression of freedom. The Union Internationale des Associations D'Alpinisme (UIAA) recently declared "Freedom for Mountaineering." As an afterthought, they added "Respect for the Mountains!" Some paraphrase this as "climb free or die." Rules exist, in some minds, only to be broken. Yet the absence of self-discipline among far too many mountain travelers has created an ever increasing number of rules about where, how and when to travel.

Gentle Expeditions

Those who venture into the mountains must discipline themselves or even more restraints will be placed on the freedom we so cherish.

The challenge we face today is to first, distinguish acceptable from unacceptable behavior, based on today's reality of increasing number and ever shrinking wilderness. While no one expects others to put lives at risk to clean up after themselves, it is reasonable to suggest that if someone can't climb an 8,000-meter peak in an ethical fashion, they climb 7,000 or 6,000-meter peaks, or climb in the Rockies, or climb in a gym. Second, we must avoid unacceptable behavior. An important starting point in determining unacceptable behavior is to learn the rules adopted by the country of destination. Nepal, for example, has long required that expeditions remove all garbage at the end of an expedition. This has been prominently displayed on every climbing permit issued at least since the early 1980's. Yet for many years, far fewer people complied with this, than ignored it. And nothing was done about it. Today, this is changing. Nepal, Pakistan and India require expeditions to pay a deposit with the promise a refund will be made if their rules are obeyed. Regardless of whether the rules promulgated by the country in which you travel have been enforced in the past or whether they will be better enforced in the future, mountain trav-

The Challenge

elers, as guests, are obligated to both learn and respect the rules. (See Appendix 1 addresses.)

Other good reference points are what our peers expect of us. The UIAA adopted this, the Kathmandu Declaration, in 1982:

> Use only technology respecting the environment its flora, its fauna and its natural resources.
>
> Reduce the negative impact of man's activities.
>
> Respect the cultural heritage and dignity of local populations.
>
> Stimulate activities which restore and rehabilitate the mountain world.
>
> Encourage contacts between mountaineers of different countries, in a spirit of friendship, mutual respect and peace.
>
> Make available all information and education necessary to improve the relationship between man and his environment.
>
> Protect effectively the mountain environment for energy needs and the disposal of waste.

Support developing countries in efforts for conservation of the environment.

Widen access to mountain regions unfettered by political considerations.

Few would disagree with the Kathmandu Declaration. Yet far too few people have ever heard of it. Even fewer have read it. More recently the UIAA adopted a Target Program for Waste Disposal. This provides more detailed guidance to what is acceptable behavior and is reproduced in its entirety in Appendix 2.

The Explorers Club, chartered in 1905, has adopted this Statement of Ethics:

"Respect the environment and local culture and leave them undisturbed. Remember that the explorer is the foreigner and the guest. Respect all local, national and international laws. Plan expeditions properly and avoid unjustified risks."

Many other guides to acceptable behavior have been published. Among the best are *Trekking Gently In The Himalayas* (see Suggested Reading). Another good source is the *Himalayan Tourist Code*, published by the Britain Tourism Concern (see Appendix 3).

The Challenge

MEETING THE CHALLENGE

Mountaineering often involves travel in developing countries. Reaching the mountains most often requires an approach through an air transportation hub. Permits must often be coordinated in the capitol cities. While it is fascinating to see these places, many mountaineers are not city people. Delhi, Kathmandu, Chengdu and Bangkok are — to some people — big, dirty cities. Yet getting to the mountains requires passing through them. The first trip to a foreign city is often fascinating, always a challenge and sometimes a real hassle.

Scott Fischer, veteran of many expeditions, climbed Everest, K-2, Lhotse, and Broad Peak without supplemental oxygen before his death on Everest in 1996. Scott used to say, "Life is life, you can go through it bumming or go through it cruising." For those who cruise, the challenges are part of the fun of being in a developing country. Those who bum often don't go back; prepare mentally to cruise rather than bum. Conserve emotional energy for when a climb or trek turns the corner and heads home. The challenges are still there. The Fischer motto still applies. Keep in mind, however, that the higher you go, the harder it is to keep cruising. Many first timers don't think this through carefully before they embark on mountain travel. Starting with the right

Gentle Expeditions

mental attitude is critical. If you can't, travel in developing countries may not be for you.

Paul Petzoldt, founder of the National Outdoor Leadership School (NOLS), is often quoted as having said "rules are for fools." Perhaps in the best of worlds, there would be no need for rules. People would all use good judgment and common sense. Unfortunately, that is not true. What Paul may have meant is that rules exist to regulate the behavior of fools who don't or can't use good judgment and common sense. It is important to know and understand what it is that a given rule is designed to accomplish, and apply it intelligently for that purpose. Rules have been promulgated because, in the past, far too many people have applied neither common sense nor good judgment. Too many people behave like fools.

Unfortunately, rules are often inconsistent. NOLS, for example, tells us that feces should be deposited no closer than 200 feet from water, mixed with dirt and buried just below the surface. *Trekking Gently in the Himalayas* tells us not to build a latrine within 50 meters of a water source and to dig holes at least 18 inches deep. Whether 200 feet or 50 meters, the distance is arbitrary. How far pathogens will leech through soil is driven by many factors, including soil type, incline and the amount of waste deposited. Rules may not make sense. For example, a permit issued by the

The Challenge

Tibet Mountaineering Association in 1992 states, "If your team has brought a toilet tent, please make sure that all holes are properly filled in and covered with heavy rocks so that animals cannot dig them up." Yet, the rule continues, "If you have not brought a toilet tent, please defecate away from streams and water sources." What difference does it make whether the hole is screened by a toilet tent as far as water pollution is concerned? The important thing is recognizing that pathogens from human waste can be a serious health risk to future climbers and local populations. The challenge is to minimize those health risks.

Some rules may even defeat their purpose. As an example, trekkers are often told to walk in single file. The challenge is to avoid destroying vegetation. If traveling through an area where there is no trail, following the rule would defeat the purpose. Hampton and Cole in *Soft Paths* advocate studying the terrain where you are traveling. If there are trails, stay on them in single file. If there are no trails, spread out and follow multiple parallel routes to minimize damage to vegetation. Stick to snowfields if there is a choice between snow and tundra. These techniques minimize impact on vegetation and allow it to recover more quickly.

Another example of a purpose-defeating rule was a proposal to ban bolting in Logan Canyon in

Utah. The purpose, or challenge, was to protect endangered plants. Yet the plants to be protected rarely grew on smooth cliff faces where bolts are used. They grew in cracks where removable protection would be placed if bolts were not used. Had bolting been banned, more removable protection would have been used, resulting in more damage to the endangered plants. After further study, the proposal was rejected.

Understanding the physical characteristics of mountains will help apply rules intelligently. Mountains are fragile ecosystems. Soils tend to be thin and easily eroded. Vegetation grows more slowly and tends to be less dense the higher one goes. As conditions become more harsh, it takes longer for soils and plants to recover from damage. It may take decades to replace vegetation or wildlife habitat torn away by boots or noisy basecamps. Although mountain ranges cover large areas, travel is often confined to narrow valleys. Good campsites with access to water and protected from rockfall and avalanches, are used over and over. Once the frequently used trails and campsites have been damaged, it still takes a lot of hard work to repair them. It is far better to avoid damage than to play catch-up after an area has been damaged. The rules, while a good starting point for meeting the challenge, are just that, a starting point.

Wild tahr beneath Pumori, Nepal. JONATHAN WATERMAN

Gentle Expeditions

Understanding the purpose of rules, knowing what our peers expect of us, applying good judgment and common sense, and having a good attitude are all just as important in meeting the challenge.

Planning

3

The key to a success for a gentle expedition is pre-departure planning. It is difficult, if not impossible, to practice sound ethics in the mountains absent good advance planning. The better the plan, the easier it will be to minimize the trace of one's passing.

DECISION MAKING

The first thing to consider is decision making. Leadership styles run the gamut from authoritarian to democratic. Each member of Herzog's expedition to Annapurna swore "to obey the leader in everything regarding the Expedition in which he may command me." Although it becomes clear in reading *Annapurna* that Herzog had been given the right to make all leadership decisions, he tried to achieve consensus in as many decisions as possible. It would be a rare climber indeed who

Gentle Expeditions

would accept less in a leader. Even if the summit team will consist of one, others will be involved in decisions. Messner first soloed Everest in 1980. Although he reached the summit alone, a companion accompanied him to his basecamp, so others were involved in making his dream a reality. Many decisions were made along the way.

The larger the group and the loftier its goal, the greater the potential for conflict as well as impact. Decide how to resolve conflicts before they arise. Ideally, as the team moves through planning and preparation to being on the mountain, they come to trust their leader. The foundation of this trust is knowing the leader will put the team's well-being first. When there is no time for discussion and consensus building, a team that trusts its leader will, more often than not, accept their leader's decision, whether they would have made the same decision or not.

I have never been asked to swear an oath as did the climbers who accompanied Herzog in 1950. As a potential example, I do send prospective team members a letter inviting them to join the expedition (see Appendix 5).

Leadership is a matter of character and style. Americans usually strive to achieve consensus in making decisions. However, most leaders usually retain the controlling vote in any decision which involves safety. If team members don't know

Planning

in advance how their leader plans to run the expedition, this may cause problems later. Make sure the team knows and is comfortable with your particular style.

THE ENVIRONMENTAL LEADER

Larger teams often appoint an experienced climbing leader. The trusted expedition leader gets through the red tape, keeps the team on track and looks after the big picture. The climbing leader focuses on the route and getting the team to the top and back. Consider designating yet another person to serve as the environmental conscience of the team. The environmental leader should remind the rest of the team of their commitment to be a gentle expedition, even when the going gets tough and others want to sacrifice that goal to reach the summit. This takes courage. Yet, when someone has been given this task by consensus before climbers get tired and the going gets tough, no one can fairly fault them for fulfilling that responsibility. The environmental leader should assume specific responsibility for planning. At the same time, they should not let the rest of the team forget that it takes hard work and commitment from every member to be a gentle expedition. Ultimately, everyone on the team must take personal responsibility for minimizing their impact.

Gentle Expeditions

SELECTING A GOAL

Some can reach the summit of any mountain and return leaving little trace of their passing. Others can't. Be realistic. Focus on satisfaction, not glory. After all, who remembers the name of the second person to climb Annapurna or, for that matter, the third to climb Everest? The point is this. While it is laudable to push one's limits, it makes no sense to select an unrealistic goal. Ambition which exceeds abilities not only magnifies risk, it virtually eliminates the prospect of minimum impact. Select a goal at the edge of your envelope, whether it be an 8,000-meter, 7,000-meter, or 6,000-meter peak, or a peak in the Rockies. Then develop a plan to avoid leaving a mess behind for someone else to clean up.

Another important factor in selecting a goal is the amount of human contact one is willing to accept. Many people go to the mountains to get away from other people. Others enjoy lots of company and feel more secure with people around. The U.S. Forest Service and National Park Service are struggling now with the concept of solitude. Studies are being done to determine the number of human interactions that are acceptable in wilderness areas. Consideration is being given to limiting the size and number of parties that will be allowed to travel in wilderness areas. If solitude is important, do not select the Abruzzi Route

Planning

on K2, or the South Col route on Everest as you will camp with many others. Nepal's current $50,000 peak fee for Everest is forcing many climbers to select smaller peaks. There are countless 6,000- and 7,000-meter peaks in the Himalayas. Many are rarely climbed. Some have never been climbed, still others don't even have names. If solitude is high on the list of desirable aspects in a trip, select one of the less popular peaks, or go in the winter rather than during the pre- or post-monsoon seasons.

Lastly, consider financial resources. The budget for a gentle expedition must include money to make that goal a reality. A working figure for planning is ten percent of the projected in-country costs, up to $2,000, for environmental purposes.

SELECTING YOUR COMPANIONS

An occasional solo trip is nice, whether it be for a few days of fishing or a back-country ski or snowshoe trip. But for anything more than a few days, most people want to be with others. Consider carefully that in almost all mountain trips, smaller is better. A small team has inherently less impact, and creates far fewer problems to deal with than a large team.

Expeditions make for strange as well as exciting times. There is often a razor thin line between pleasure and pain. People are in unfamiliar sur-

Gentle Expeditions

roundings, suffering altitude headaches, and undergoing the stress of intense effort. Emotions run high. Some thrive on the stress. Others don't. Marriages fail, people get in fist fights. Often enough, expeditions destroy friendships. Some don't even talk to people they climbed with more than 50 years ago. If you look to the mountains to restore your soul, nothing could be worse than going to the mountains with people who don't get along with one another. People who engage in verbal violence can destroy a team. Stacey Allison, first American woman to summit Everest, in her book *Beyond The Limits*, says she chose her team for K2 based on their ability to get along. "Good climbers are a dime a dozen; people who can work in a team are rare." Choose your companions carefully. Otherwise, emotional disaster is sure to result.

SELECTING GEAR

Bright colors are the style in adventure gear; orange parkas, yellow tents, chartreuse webbing, etc., etc. There are times when bright makes sense. It is much easier to spot a lost or injured climber wearing a bright parka. Other times, bright is unnecessary. Tents in earth tones blend in better than reds or oranges. The same is true for lots of other gear that needn't be bright for safety reasons. Visual pollution detracts from others'

Planning

enjoyment of remote areas. Consider how to decrease it whenever possible. Give the selection of colors in personal and group gear careful thought.

HOMEWORK

Commercial travel guides are available for almost every place on earth there are mountains. Select a good travel guide early in planning. These guides are a good source of information about cultural and religious issues. Beyond travel guides, people who have just returned from an area are an excellent resource. Talk to as many people who have been to your destination as possible. Contact the land manager, park headquarters or other governmental body that issues permits and ask about special projects such as trail restoration. Learning about the history, customs and, for those with an aptitude for it, the language, adds dramatically to the quality of mountain travel. People really appreciate hearing "hello" and "thank you" in their language.

Check with a traveler's clinic to determine what inoculations are recommended and any special health risks in the area. Over 50 countries require visitors to present the results of tests for HIV before entry. The U.S. State Department will provide a current list and specific requirements upon request. Plan to take syringes, needles and a transfusion kit in your medical gear as these

Gentle Expeditions

items are often reused in developing countries. Condoms may be of questionable quality in developing countries. Bring them from home. Use latex rather than animal skins as the latter may be penetrated by certain viruses. Appendix 4 contains a list of all the items mentioned related to gentle expeditions. Use it as a planning guide.

Both the American Alpine Club (AAC) and the American Mountain Foundation (AMF) ask climbers to prepare post-expedition reports. These reports are excellent resources for future expeditions. The AAC has one of the best mountain research libraries in the world. It is available to the public for in-person research (call ahead), and to AAC members for both in-person research and telephone inquiries (see Appendix 1).

THE A-TEAM

An A-team consists of people who can be trusted to do things right. They should form the core of the staff that is hired to support a gentle expedition. After a few trips to the Himalayas or other ranges, people know who they can trust and rely on them to form the A-team on future trips. First time travelers don't have this advantage. A good way to pick an A-team is to ask others who they have used, what problems they experienced and how they suggest avoiding those problems. The American Alpine Club and similar organiza-

Planning

tions are fine sources of information. As discussed later, a good A-team can play an important role in pre-departure planning. It pays to identify the A-team as early as possible.

Wages paid to a sirdar (staff leader), cooks, porters, yak handlers and others who form the staff of an expedition are a critically important source of income in most mountain areas. There is no shortage of people who want to work in the mountains. It is a buyer's market. Messner has proposed forming guide associations in the Himalayas similar to those in Europe, Canada and the United States. Such groups would ensure the high-altitude porters who risk their lives carrying loads are properly trained and paid a fair wage for the often dangerous work they do. Unions did spring up in Nepal after the 1993 elections. If Messner's idea works, guides and porters will have a vested interest in preserving the mountains, just as do the professional guides who require their clients follow the rules in the Grand Canyon, on Denali and Mt. Rainier. They will know what to do and how to do it with minimum impact. Until then, be a selective consumer. Anyone who applies for work should know your goals and, perhaps more importantly, that full pay depends on meeting your standards. Discussing this up front and getting such a commitment is a critical first step. This should apply to everyone on the staff, from sirdar

Gentle Expeditions

to yak herder.

Plan so it is possible for the entire staff to meet those goals. It is all too easy to say there won't be any campfires. The cook will use a kerosene stove to heat "bed tea" in the morning. After hot tea, trekkers emerge from a down sleeping bag, then put on a fleece sweater and Gore-tex jacket before facing the morning chill — no camp fire required. Historically, however, hired staff have come to expect camp fires. While the times are changing with the formation of the Trekking Workers Association of Nepal and similar unions, porters still are often barefoot and wear only ragged cotton pants, a shirt and a vest. They may bring nothing for protection from the rain or snow other than a scrap of plastic.

Child labor is another issue to consider. The International Labor Organization asserts that children under the age of 15 should not be employed except in light work. Very little work on an expedition qualifies as light. Though many countries have child labor laws, the use of child labor remains widespread in the Himalayas. A gentle expedition is no place for a child. All will work hard, sometimes in dangerous conditions. Yet often women are often paid less than men for doing the same work. Budget so that everyone can be paid the same wage for the same work, regardless of age or sex.

Tibetan child near Nylam in 1992. TOM LEECH

Gentle Expeditions

Trekking rules in many countries now require porters be provided with a stove and kerosene for cooking. Despite this, they will want to cook over a wood fire during the expedition. They can then sell the stove and take the kerosene home. If you really want to avoid the use of fires, you must not only provide the stove and fuel, you must insist they are used. After the team is in their sleeping bags, the staff will want a fire to keep warm. If you don't want porters to sleep by a fire, plan to provide them blankets and tarps. Provide climbing staff with the same tents, sleeping bags and foam pads the team will use. Budget enough money to provide the right gear so the entire staff can be part of a gentle expedition.

Go Light!

Take what is needed, nothing more. This is another of those, easy enough to say, harder to sort out issues. Everyone has a different view of what this means. What some view as essential, others may see as excess. The authors of *Wilderness Ethics* compare packs to Mae West and Twiggy: "Some people carry more than you can possibly use on a two- or three-day weekend; others less than you need to enjoy a reasonably good time." Mae West packs accommodate the needs of the wearer, and may provide an extra pair of mittens for another team member whose hands

Planning

get cold. Twiggy packs match the "go light" idea. Expeditions are just an expansion of this discussion. How light or heavy an expedition goes is a question of style. Just remember, a Mae West style will generate more problems to anticipate and solve.

Regardless of what is brought, pack to generate as little garbage as possible. The German Alpine Club (DAV) fields hundreds of treks every year. Among the first things a DAV trekker receives is a letter with a bright orange garbage bag telling them all of their garbage must fit in the bag. Theoretically, the bag is brought back to Germany afterward the trip. The bag is a good way to get people thinking, before they leave, about how to reduce the amount of garbage they will generate on a trip. While this gets people thinking, like everything else, it requires follow through. The National Park Service fined the DAV $350 in 1985 when their orange garbage bags were found abandoned at 17,000 feet on Denali.

There are many ways to minimize packing material. Plan on buying as much food as possible locally. This supports the host country's economy, dispenses with superfluous western packaging and allows you the cultural experience of shopping in local markets. Plan to buy cereals and vegetables in bulk. Pack what is bought in cloth bags or woven baskets. As the food is used,

Gentle Expeditions

bags or baskets can be put to other uses until they biodegrade.

After traveling halfway around the world, no one wants to cancel an expedition for want of potatoes. Rely on the A-team to verify what food and other goods can be purchased locally. Send them a list with specific items early in the planning process. Tell them to advise what will not be available. Then buy at home only what they can't get. This not only reduces shipping costs, it helps avoid the common criticism that very few dollars spent by tourists go to the benefit of local economies. After all, developing countries are dependent on tourism. Putting money directly into the hands of local grocers and shopkeepers is the way to support local economies. Plan to shop in Kathmandu, Lhasa, Islamabad, New Delhi, Cusco, or similar cities rather than remote villages.

Plan to avoid taking polystyrene packing bits on an expedition. All too often, they blow away. The result is a multi-day clean-up effort. Plastic "bubble wrap" is also a potential problem because it melts instead of burning, and leaves a sticky mess. Burning plastic also gives off toxic gasses. It doesn't make a good gift because there isn't any use for it in developing countries. Even the most fragile gear can be packed in a sleeping bag in a five gallon plastic bucket.

Lots of other packaging can be left at home as

Planning

well. The less brought, the less to deal with in lands where "pack it in, pack it out" means bringing it home. As an example, in 1990, a well known photographer came into Everest Basecamp carrying a large black plastic garbage bag over his shoulder. He asked the leader of a clean-up expedition what he should do with the bag full of empty film boxes. The leader told him: haul it out and next time, take the film out of the boxes before leaving home! A lot of stuff comes in packaging that is designed to sell the product, not make it any easier or safer to pack. Get rid of all but absolutely essential packaging before leaving. Consolidate everything possible into bulk packages.

Related to packaging is the issue of paper and plastic eating utensils. Metal plates, bowls, etc. are readily available and inexpensive in developing countries. Again, rely on the A-team to confirm what is available and plan to avoid the potential waste stream that paper and plastic create. Plan to buy at least two times the number of team members to account for loss and "down time" during washing.

Toxic wastes require special attention. This includes anything that will create health hazards in addition to aesthetic problems. Examples include medical waste, fuel and batteries. All toxic wastes must be carried out to an appropriate disposal facility. Often that means bringing them back home. While a battery seems harmless enough, outer casings eventually disintegrate. Heavy metals are left behind. Remember the first rule, go light.

Does everyone need a tape player? Could the team get by without a boombox? Consider having tentmates share a Walkman with two headphones. Plan to use rechargeable batteries. Solar panels work great for recharging batteries. With some planning, light can be provided using low watt bulbs; even a boombox will work on a solar panel and battery system. Good sources for information, panels and related gear include The Real Goods Trading Company and The Wisdom Light Group (see Appendix 1). Test the entire system before leaving to make it works properly. Bring a repair kit. If the budget will allow it, plan to donate the solar panels to a village on the way home.

Someday, basecamp tents may incorporate solar panels. Until then, think carefully about batteries of all kinds. Are they really needed? Will solar work in their place? Minimize what is brought and develop a plan to collect all batteries as they are used and bring them home.

Kerosene lanterns are a great alternative to battery-powered lanterns. Lanterns and kerosene can be bought almost anywhere. On most trips, kerosene will also be the main fuel for cooking for all but extremely high altitude. One of the chal-

Planning

lenges of using liquid fuel is the risk of spills. Fuel often must be transferred from 55-gallon drums to smaller containers to stoves. While spills won't have the impact of the *Exxon Valdez*, plan to minimize the impact of the spills that do inevitably occur. Funnels are essential. Buy shallow metal pans which can be filled with sand or dirt. Pour fuel over these pans. As fuel builds up in the pan, it can be burned.

Butane cartridges still seem to be the most dependable rig for high altitude use. I am still embarrassed about a 1987 expedition: we were so relieved to have survived a series of epics we threw unused cartridges in our post-expedition bonfire. The explosions were hilarious at the time and helped relieve tension. But metal doesn't burn.

Plan to bring out cartridges, used and unused. There is a market for full ones at gear shops in many places. Plan to bring empties out to a proper disposal area. Ask the A-team before leaving if such an area exists. If not, plan to bring empties back home.

Glass is another important factor in packing. While glass is not toxic, it is definitely a hazard and has no place on an expedition. With planning, everything from hot sauce to liquor can be packed in reusable plastic. The Nalge Company (see Appendix 1) is a great source for everything

Gentle Expeditions

from five gallon to half ounce plastic containers. Ask them to send a catalog and plan to make maximum use of alternatives to glass. Some object to plastic, however, plastic bottles are valuable to people in developing countries. Broken glass is not.

Try as you might, garbage will still pile up. Estimate before leaving how much garbage the trip will generate and plan to haul it out. One option is to bring garbage bags from home. Heavy woven plastic bags such as those sold by The Bag Connection (see Appendix 1) work well. Another alternative is burlap bags, used for everything in developing countries. Burlap is more durable than plastic, is reusable, and will biodegrade. Ask to A-team to verify that burlap bags are available and what they cost.

Remember in planning that much of what we consider garbage is reusable in developing countries, such as aluminum cans, plastic buckets, plastic bottles. Organized recycling is happening in India, Tibet and Nepal. Ask the A-team before leaving what can be recycled locally. Plan to collect those items and carry them out to the recycling center. If recyclable items end up in the common garbage pile, mixed with food scraps and snow, they become garbage.

HUMAN WASTE

Each day, a healthy adult generates a pound,

Boy collecting recyclables, Shegar, Tibet, 1990. STEVE KIN

more or less, of solid waste. This has led to the determination that human waste should be deposited in the infamous blue plastic bags issued by National Park Service Rangers on Mt. Rainier. The bags are then deposited in receptacles on the mountain. Receptacles are removed each fall by helicopter. The waste is then transported to an incinerator. This is an expensive proposition and, at least in the author's view, totally impracticable in a developing country.

There were about 400 people in the Everest Basecamp in Nepal in May, 1993. At a pound per person per day, that is a lot of human waste. More than 10,000 people trek in the Khumbu valley in a typical year. That is five tons of human waste a day being deposited in a valley with no septic systems. Feces do not decompose at high altitude. The precise altitude at which decomposition stops is uncertain. The 1990 Everest Environmental Expedition reopened a pit toilet used during a 1987 expedition in the Basecamp at 17,000 feet and did not see that there had been any decomposition in three years.

People in many developing countries use flowing water as a natural sewer system. The risk of doing as they do is that our guts contain bugs their systems may not be used to. Our feces create a real health risk in such an environment. As half the world's people depend on mountains for

Planning

their water, every expedition needs to plan for dealing with human waste so it will not foul water supplies.

The 1992 Everest Environmental Expedition tested water at the Rongbuk Monastery, the river and at a spring in the basecamp. Tests at all three sites showed positive results for coliform bacteria, an indication that water above 16,800 feet in the Rongbuk valley is contaminated with human waste.

Consider using portable potties. They can be made from five gallon plastic buckets with tight sealing lids. Such buckets are used for paint and bulk foods and are readily available in the United States. They are good for packing fragile items and are recyclable. Make a seat out of plywood large enough to cover the bucket. Cut a hole in the center, cover the rough edges with duct tape, and cover the wood with foam from an old sleeping pad.

One bucket will hold about 40 pounds of waste. Contrary to legend, in 1992, Tibetan yak herders agreed to pack these buckets on their yaks once they understood the buckets would not leak. Even better, farmers were perfectly willing to deposit our waste on their fields, again contrary to legend. Throwing the bucket in with the deal made the offer irresistible. Human waste has been used as fertilizer for centuries in places like Japan and Korea. Plants grown in such environments are perfectly safe to eat, so long as they are washed carefully and cooked.

Multiply the number of people by the number of days trekking and divide by 40 to calculate how many buckets will be needed. Then throw in a few extra. Don't urinate in the buckets. Urine can defoliate plants so try to urinate on rocks. Put all toilet paper, tampons, etc. in a separate bucket or bag. Buy some lime to keep the smell down. Discuss the plan with porters, donkey drivers or yak herders before hiring them. Show them how the system works and explain that they will get some of the buckets. The key is rounding up the buckets and making a simple seat before leaving home.

If the plan will be to bury human waste, read *How to Shit in the Woods*. The author advocates using shallow individual "cat holes" rather than a group hole. Select areas away from water sources and well above the high water mark in areas subject to higher levels during runoffs or floods. Stir the feces with dirt to encourage faster decomposition. Keep in mind that this is not a viable plan for camps that will be occupied for extended periods of time.

Over the long term, solar toilets might be the best solution for disposing of human waste in such camps. These are not composting toilets. They do not need oxygen, fodder, chemicals or water to work. Until such technology is perfected, consider the porta-potty system. Chances are, however, a different plan will be needed for basecamp. Bring a shovel and a pick. More about this in Chapter Four.

Above basecamp is another story. The good news is that the higher climbers go, the fewer people there are to deal with and the less time they are there. The bad news is that if high camp is on a popular route, there may still be a lot of people. The blue bag system used at Mt. Rainier isn't practical unless there is an incinerator nearby. The best system in high camps in developing countries is probably to use a crevasse as a toilet. Remember which side of camp is the "pooper." Be sure to get snow to melt for water from the other side. Even then, the great unknown is which side the preceding party used for which purpose. Fresh snow will cover the evidence. This makes the old "don't eat yellow snow" test risky at best. Bring enough iodine to sterilize all water, even snow you melt. Iodine solution seems to work best as, while it takes 20 minutes to kill the "bugs," there is no additional wait for tablets to dissolve. Regardless of the system, bring bags to collect toilet paper and feminine hygiene products.

Many villages beneath tree line use effective compost producing toilets. These are often built on a hill or raised platform. A pile of leaves

Indian outhouse below Kanchenjunga.. BOB MCCONNELL

Planning

are usually found nearby. Proper protocol is to throw a handful of leaves on top of each deposit; there is often a bottle or bucket of water easily accessible.

Local people wash themselves after using the toilet, with their left hand. This gives rise to the tradition that the right hand is clean and the left hand dirty. Never give or receive food with your left hand in the Himalayas.

If compost is being recovered from the toilet, there will be a trap door near the bottom of one wall. Compost is removed and used for fertilizer. Avoid putting anything in such toilets other than human waste. Regardless of whether local toilets, portable toilets or cat holes are used, plan to burn toilet paper where it is feasible and carry out all feminine hygiene materials.

SUPPLEMENTAL OXYGEN

The question of whether or not to use supplemental oxygen while climbing the 8,000-meter peaks has been hotly debated since portable systems were developed in the 1920s. In 1922, Edward Norton and Howard Somervell from Mallory's team reached 28,000 feet climbing without supplemental oxygen. That same year, Mallory said, "when I think of mountaineering with four cylinders of oxygen on one's back and a mask on one's face, well, it loses its charm." Yet when Mallory and

Gentle Expeditions

Irving were last seen by Odell "going strong for the summit," both had bottles of oxygen on their backs.

Medical doctors calculated that no one could reach the summit of the 8,000-meter peaks and survive without supplemental oxygen. This theory was debunked by Messner and Peter Habeler on May 8, 1978, when they reached the summit of Everest without using bottled oxygen and returned. Climbing the highest peaks without supplemental oxygen does take those who attempt it to the very limit of their capabilities. Tales of disembodied spirits joining those who climb without supplemental oxygen go back to the earliest expeditions. Frank Smythe, a member of the 1933 British expedition to Everest, made a solo summit attempt without supplemental oxygen. After returning from 28,100 feet on the North Face, he described feeling he was accompanied by a second person. He told of dividing a mint cake and offering half to his non-existent companion. Stephen Venables recounts that in May 1988, after reaching the summit of Everest without supplemental oxygen, he sensed being joined during his solo bivouac above the South Summit by Doug Scott's son Mike, Eric Shipton and other spirits from the past.

Hardly a beer is drunk by climbers without someone blaming their memory loss on too much time at high altitude. Dr. John West in his book *Everest, the Testing Place*, asserts that memory loss, although demonstrable immediately after returning from a high altitude expedition, recovers fully within a year or so. He doesn't address how this sorts out if one goes on expeditions every year. Memory loss aside, climbing the 8,000-meter peaks without supplemental oxygen is serious business. While it allows climbing alpine style, that is, carrying everything from one camp to the next and then making a dash for the summit, it increases the risk. We all take risks in climbing, just as we do driving to work. As rational people, we try to reduce risks to an acceptable level. Peter Hackett in his classic *Mountain Sickness* explains that all of us adapt to altitude differently. The same person may even adapt slower on one trip than on previous trips. Until you have climbed above 20,000 feet, there is no way to know how your body will react, much less evaluate the risk of climbing the highest peaks without oxygen.

Climbers hotly debate whether using supplemental oxygen is appropriate for them or their team. Whether or not to use supplemental oxygen is a question of style. Just the same, the decision to use "O's" gives rise to an ethical obligation to bring out all the bottles this style generates. The Ministry of Tourism in Nepal now requires expeditions produce the same number of oxygen bottles they take to Everest for inspection before their environmental deposit is returned. Sadly, a secondary market in used oxygen bottles has already sprung

Gentle Expeditions

up in Kathmandu. Those who can't bring their bottles down from the South Col or higher can buy empty bottles to meet their quota at the Ministry of Tourism. If this secondary market disappears, then climbers who elect to use "O's" will be forced to bring back the bottles.

Out of five summit climbers, three people from the 1994 Sagarmatha Environmental Expedition reached the summit without using "O's." The expedition initiated a "buy back" program to bring their own and other oxygen bottles back from the South Col of Everest. High-altitude porters were paid $6 for each bottle brought down to Basecamp. Over 250 bottles, or about one-fourth of those littering the South Col, were returned to Basecamp and brought back to the United States. Under the direction of Brent Bishop, this buy back program continued in 1995 and 1996. If the team will use bottled oxygen, budget enough money to pay the staff to bring every bottle down and out to Kathmandu.

The better the plan, the easier it will be to conduct a gentle expedition. Regardless of how elaborate the planning, it won't succeed unless everyone on the team and the entire staff supports it. As the plan is developed, it will need to be a major topic of pre-departure discussion, revision and final approval by the team. The plan can then be presented when hiring staff as a "take it or leave it" part of the hiring process.

In The Field

4

Between the idea, and the reality, between the motion and the act, falls the shadow. Between the conception and the creation, between the emotion and the response falls the shadow.
—T.S. Eliot

Arrival

So, the planning is done. Rest on the plane, knowing a great deal has already been accomplished. The goal is realistic. The team is in good spirits and works well together. The challenges are clear. A solid plan is in place for minimizing impact. Only the food that can't be bought locally has been brought along. Packaging is near non-existent. The A-team has arranged everything else. You will be in a radically different world when you land. Reminding the team of its commitment to leave as little trace as possible should be a constant process until back home. The higher one goes, the tougher

Gentle Expeditions

it gets. Now will fall the shadow.

The number one priority on arrival is staying healthy. Sick people are too miserable to focus on much. They quickly lose enthusiasm for accomplishing all but critical tasks. Each team member should select a medical "buddy" in which they can confide. Disclose to each other any allergies, and any medication taken. It is especially important that anyone who provides medical care know what meds are on board the patient. A medical buddy should be able to provide this information if you can't. If this is impractical, record all drugs taken in your expedition diary.

Do not share water bottles, pipes, etcetera with anyone until the trip is over. Purify all water unless you actually see a mineral water bottle opened. Wash your hands as often as possible and before every meal. Wait until the trip home to sample food from street vendors. Stick with milder dishes in the restaurants. Remember every taxi will have bald tires, dysfunctional gauges and the driver will look like he is 14. Learn how to say "slow down"; if that doesn't work, get out. Bottom line — avoid taxis and walk whenever possible, and practice safe sex. Those who ignore this advice do so at their peril. Not much is worse than setting out on a long expedition, or even a short trek, with stomach problems, a neck brace or venereal disease.

In The Field

SUPERVISING THE STAFF

As observed earlier, a common excuse for unethical expeditionary behavior is that local people don't care. Well, the same holds true for the U.S. But in other countries, we should care because we are guests — in their home — essentially. All too often the porter who throws a candy wrapper on the trail learned that behavior by watching our predecessors. The buck stops with the boss who hires these people. The boss is responsible for every employees' conduct. You are the boss.

Rely on the A-team to hire other staff. Emphasize that the A-team must explain how the expedition will work to each person who is hired and require that each agree to support minimum impact mountaineering. While important, this is just the starting point. Provide all staff the equipment needed to be part of a gentle expedition. Most importantly, set a good example.

Many issues will require supervision. Three are critical. Insist the staff actually use the stoves and fuel provided for them. See that they don't leave a trail of litter in their path. Convince them to use the porta-potty. Such issues are best approached by setting proper examples. Giving up campfires, abstaining from littering, picking up litter along the trail and using the toilet system will set the right example. Rest assured the staff will closely observe how the team behaves. If the

Gentle Expeditions

team is lax, expect the staff to ignore the plan completely. "Do as I say, not as I do," never works.

Another priority is the trust and rapport established with the staff. Start by learning to properly pronounce their names. If you can't understand when they say their name, ask them or the sirdar to write it down. Calling the cook and the cook's helper by name will do a great deal to get that person on the A-team. Make a point of learning a new word of their language every day. Write down the ones used often. Teach them one word a day from your language as well. Respect their knowledge of the area and their traditions. You'll like the results.

THE APPROACH

An approach march is an excellent way to both acclimatize and gain strength. It is a time to be savored as the team comes together. This is also the time to verify how well the local systems for disposal of rubbish identified during the planning phase really work. Recent years have seen the construction of rubbish dumps along many popular trekking routes. The Sagarmatha Pollution Control Committee (SPCC) now operates incinerators in both Lukla and Namche Bazaar in the Khumbu Valley. Coordinate with the person in control such systems. It may be possible to leave some money

In The Field

with the understanding that they will pay your porters, yak, camel or truck drivers when they return with rubbish as discussed below.

Use burlap or heavy plastic bags to collect refuse along the route. If the approach is too trashed to clean, clean a perimeter around each camp. It makes no sense to carry what is collected up on the approach. As supplies are used, decrease the size of the staff. Pay them to haul back collected rubbish. They must understand they will not be paid until they arrive at a designated location with the rubbish. It will probably be necessary to send back one of the A-team with payment.

Many approaches today follow tea houses where one can find hot tea, a beer, a place to sleep and a shower. Use your own mug and spoon in tea houses. Determine what is readily available or already on the stove rather than ask for something that needs to be cooked anew — this saves firewood. Never throw anything in your host's fire without first asking permission.

When a shower is needed, look for a tea house that uses the "back burner" system developed by the Annapurna Conservation Area Project. This system of pipes heats water anytime the fire is burning. Better yet, look for a tea house using a solar hot water system. Consumer dollars are best spent supporting those who are actually trying to meet the challenge.

Gentle Expeditions

    Consider avoiding the tea house shower scene entirely. Look for a waterfall, a quiet stream, or a natural hot spring for bathing. While this may save a tree otherwise used to heat the water, remember this is someone's drinking water. Get wet, leave the water. Soap up and rinse off with a bucket of water. Then go back in the water for a final rinse. Use biodegradable soap. Ask how the local people bathe. Men and women in Nepal, Tibet and India do not expose themselves, even while bathing. Men keep their shorts on; women bathe under a loose smock. Respect their modesty by adopting the same tricks.

    Avoiding stomach troubles during the approach will aid in acclimatization. Make certain everyone who touches food or the dishes in which food is cooked and served washes their hands with a scrub brush and a germicide such as Phisohex. Show the staff how to wash dishes to reduce risk of sickness.

    One technique is to heat the water while rounding up everything that needs washing — move away from the drinking water source. The hot water goes into a metal or plastic wash basin. Add biodegradable soap and use a sturdy scrub brush. Wash sharp knives first, then cups and bowls, plates and silverware. Pots and pans last. As each item is washed, it goes still soapy into a

In The Field

second empty wash basin to drain. Rinse with hot clean water. Pour the rinse water through a large strainer. Food scraps from the strainer go either into the porta-potty or a five gallon plastic bucket reserved for compost. Dry everything and then cover or put it away.

RESPECTING LOCAL PEOPLE

A critical part of being a gentle expedition is respecting local people and their traditions. Always give porters with heavy loads the right of way. Avoid loud behavior as it often offends local people. No boomboxes on the trail. Use ear phones or low volume. Once out of the cities in the Himalayas, there are few adult beggars. Children beg even in the most remote villages. They beg for pictures of the Dalai Lama in Tibet for pens in India and for candy in Nepal. Responding to these beautiful young spirits can have unexpected consequences. In Tibet, you may find yourself under arrest or being escorted to the border by some of the Chinese Army's finest. No one wants to do time over a Dalai Lama picture. At the Tibet border, Chinese guards often thumb through books looking for forbidden pictures concealed between the pages.

Apart from Chinese insecurity that some Tibetan child's ultimate dream might be fulfilled, responding to children who beg rewards their behavior, encourages begging by other children, and cultivates a mentality of dependence. Parents are often embarrassed by such behavior. Far better to arrive in a village and seek out a teacher or other responsible adult. Present them gifts for later distribution to children. Bring magic slates, writing paper, crayons, pens, toothbrushes and toothpaste and vitamins. Candy causes tooth decay. An inflatable globe is a great way to strike up a conversation and is an excellent gift. Showing pictures of family and home are another great way to start conversations.

Going to the bathroom is a very private experience for people in the Himalayas. During eight trips to Nepal, three to Tibet and two to India, I have rarely seen local people or staff go to the bathroom. They are very discreet. Modesty is obviously compromised to some extent by having one designated place for the toilet. This is reduced somewhat by surrounding it with a privacy-wind-snow-and rain screen. Placing the porta-potty behind rocks or bushes and well away from the center of camp will help. Explaining the process and the goal is critical.

Neither men nor women should wear revealing attire. The Kathmandu Environmental Education Project asserts the most appropriate dress for women is a loose-fitting light cotton dress. These are readily available in most bazaars. Men

In The Field

get away with more abbreviated attire; however, shirts should always be worn. Again, loose-fitting light cotton pants and shirts are readily available and inexpensive. These also make good souvenirs, assuming they have not been totally trashed during the trip.

Stone cairns dot many valleys in such profusion they no longer have any meaning as trail markers. Special consideration should be given before adding to existing trail markers and cairns. Even on the highest glaciers, wands are often found which mark some forgotten trail used by previous climbers. Give those who will follow the opportunity to do their own route finding. When leaving an area, recover any wands and destroy any cairns you erected to mark a route. Note any sightings of rare animals and report them to the appropriate land manager on return. Such reports help determine the environmental "health" of remote areas. Respect religious shrines and artifacts. Leave mani stones and prayer flags untouched. What may be considered a nice souvenir by a visitor may have deep religious significance to its owner. The bazaar, not the trail, is the place to collect souvenirs.

BASECAMP

By now, the goal is in sight. The realization the team is about to get on a rope together will charge

Gentle Expeditions

everyone with adrenaline. This is a critical time. The discipline established during the approach can be quickly lost if focus shifts immediately to the climb. Take off the heavy boots and put on sandals or tennis shoes. This will not only rest the feet, it will avoid unnecessary damage to vegetation and soils (if any). Select tent sites away from any vegetation.

The toughest issue to address will be disposing of human waste. Assuming this was under control during the approach, it will be difficult to regain control if it is lost now. People will need to go to the bathroom as soon as they arrive. Immediately identify one location for that purpose. Failing to do this will lead to a profusion of small piles "hidden" here and there with resulting smell, flies and health hazards. The ideal location will be protected from rock fall, out of the wind, out of sight from camp proper, have a great view, and will not pollute basecamp or down valley water sources. Make the facility as comfortable and private as possible to encourage its use.

If a porta-potty was used on the approach and there is a nearby village that will accept the addition of human waste and food scraps to their fields, this system can be used in basecamp. Give it a try. The government of Nepal is now flirting with requiring this in Everest basecamp. It is an idea whose time has come. If porta potties are not feasible, dig

In The Field

a pit toilet in the designated location. Whether it be a pit toilet or a porta-potty, this should also be the dump for kitchen wastes. Encourage its use.

Typically, most of the staff will stay in basecamp until the climb is completed. The team will descend to basecamp for R&R during the climb. Since the team will be short-term visitors, the camp should be set up to recognize this reality and reduce the the staff's long-term impact. Set up systems that will enable the staff to occupy basecamp, perhaps for months, without trashing it. The sirdar should understand he will be held responsible for supervising those who remain in basecamp.

The first way to reduce impact and costs will be to cut staff to the absolute minimum, perhaps keeping only the sirdar, cook, and cook's helper. Either fetch transportation for the return by runner when needed, or arrange a specific time for the porters, yak drivers, camels or jeeps to return. Before they leave, this group should be paid to thoroughly police the camp, picking up all rubbish and loading it into plastic or burlap bags. Provided there is a suitable refuse dump on their route home, the porters should be paid to carry out the rubbish they collect. Promise payment when the rubbish arrives at the designated locations as discussed above. If it wasn't possible to work out payment with someone reliable at the designated site during the approach, send the money with someone

Gentle Expeditions

from the A-team. The risk of handling this any other way is the porters will carry the rubbish only until they disappear from sight and then dump it.

The first few days in basecamp are often spent resting from the approach, acclimatizing and reconnoitering. Use this time to evaluate how close the team came to leaving no trace on the approach. Discuss how to do better on the way out, especially if there were unanticipated problems. Record the condition of basecamp on arrival, both on film and in writing. Coordinate with any other teams in the area. Share with them your goals as a gentle expedition. Enlist their cooperation. Establish a place to collect recyclable materials, a place to collect burnables, and a dump for all other trash. These sites should be clearly marked for each purpose. Explain the system to the sirdar. Protect each site from the wind or stuff will blow all over. Ideally, each site will be protected from rain and snow as well (blue plastic tarps are ideal). This is critical for burning — it is hard enough to keep a fire going at 16,000 feet, even with leftover kerosene, but it is impossible to burn a soggy mess. The best way to handle burnables is to burn them as they accumulate and while still dry.

Climbers have told each other for years that people in the Himalayas believe large fires will bring bad storms. As a result, the bonfire is usually not started until the climb is over. Indeed, in

In The Field

1987, within 24 hours after torching our accumulated trash in mid-expedition, Tibet experienced its biggest snow storm in many years. Having spoken to many Indian, Tibetan and Nepali people since, it is clear they are not opposed to all fires. After all, they burn wood and dung to cook food and heat tea. Many are offended, however, by burning things that will pollute the air such as plastic and meat wrappings. Inquire about and respect what are often religious-based beliefs.

Locate the pan and dirt system used to catch fuel spills close to the fuel storage area so that it will be used. Set up another pan near the kitchen and insist that kitchen stoves be refilled there rather than in the kitchen. Show the cook how to use the fire extinguisher. As on the approach, the example set during this critical time will go a long way towards determining whether the plan is followed by the staff after the team starts up the mountain.

Initiate a "buy back" program for staff who remain in basecamp. Expect to pay porters about $2 for each ten kilos of rubbish collected in and around basecamp. This has multiple advantages: making use of a labor force otherwise unoccupied; reinforcing a "leave no trace" ethic in their minds; and most importantly, rewarding people with cash to put into the local economy.

Backhauling rubbish, Tibet, 1990. TUI DE ROY

In The Field

Initially, staff can be paid for specific types of rubbish, such as ten kilos of metal or ten kilos of glass. This helps in separating recyclables. Toward the end, as rubbish becomes scarce, mixed bags should be accepted.

High Camps

The higher a climb, the more difficult it is to minimize impact. The good news is that fewer people go high. Fewer numbers mean less impact. Now is the time for patience and good judgment. Find the fun to be had in waiting out bad weather. Putting the team at risk courts disaster. Dealing with a disaster or even an injury virtually eliminates the chance of minimizing impact. If hauling loads to establish fixed camps, the logical solution is to haul rubbish down on return trips. This becomes a real mind game. It is easy enough to promise this before carrying up a heavy load. It is an entirely different thing after a long carry to hoist up a pack just as heavy as the one just put down. Offer high-altitude porters a buy back program similar to that used in basecamp. The pay should reflect both the increased exertion and danger of working at higher altitudes. Five oxygen bottles can increase a porter's daily wage by $30.

I do not know of any Himalayan expedition that has carried human waste down from a climb.

Gentle Expeditions

Blue bags are impractical when there is not an incinerator at basecamp. The accepted solution at high camps is to designate a toilet area over a crevasse or on one side of a ridge so that the other side of the ridge has clean snow to melt for water. Remember to iodine water in case previous teams have fouled the snow. Use wands to mark the toilet.

Many teams fix rope between camps, allowing rapid descent for bad weather or in an emergency. Many fixed ropes have been abandoned. On popular routes, this has led to spaghetti-like tangles of old, deteriorating ropes. This robs those who will follow of the route-finding opportunities; old ropes are often unsafe too. More teams now are climbing in alpine style — carrying everything on their backs from one camp to the next, both up and back down the mountain. This is a question of style — like using bottled oxygen. If the style chosen includes fixed ropes, you owe it to those who will follow to remove them — like removing oxygen bottles. The same applies to ladders and other aid.

Think before aid is put in whether it is necessary and how difficult it will be to recover. Bring as much off the mountain as possible in such a way as not to put anyone at unnecessary risk.

As a practical matter, fixed ropes and other aids are left to be brought out by the last people

Fixed rope on the Abruzzi Route, K2. CHARLEY MACE

Gentle Expeditions

down. But a summit team will be whipped. On early attempts in the Himalayas, support teams "backed up" the summit team and were available to help out in an emergency. Alpine-style climbing sometimes has disastrous consequences, such as on K-2 when six climbers died in 1995. Had a back up team been waiting to help, the effort to reach the summit might not have cost their lives. The fresher members of a backup team are the logical ones to remove fixed rope and other gear as the team leaves the mountain.

So do you climb alpine-style and minimize impact and trash, potentially increasing risk with a lack of support? Or do you climb in a more classic style using siege tactics? The latter provides the support to climb safer yet simultaneously, by the weight of a larger team, has a greater environmental impact on the mountain. These are questions best answered according to the needs and abilities of each climbing team.

HEADING HOME

While most teams plan to return together, all too often team members depart piecemeal. Sometimes this is a result of sickness or injury. Other times, members reach their limit and quit before stronger members are ready to leave. Heading home must be planned and executed as carefully as the earlier phases of a trip. Account for early

Everest from Kalapatar, 18,000 feet. JONATHAN WATERMAN

departures and other unexpected events. Even with a good plan, the combination of exhaustion and relief if there has been an epic may well negate all the good work that has preceded. Rely on what is hopefully by now an expanded A-team. It will be clear almost at once on return to basecamp how well placed such reliance will be. Hopefully, human waste and kitchen scraps will either be in buckets ready for transportation out or in a pit toilet. Burnables will either have been burned or will be dry and ready to burn. Recycleables will be collected and ready to pack. Toxics will be packed separately. Transportation out, porters, yaks, ponies or whatever, will either be there or on the way. If, on the other hand, rubbish and human waste is scattered about, a tough time lies ahead. Whatever condition, leave basecamp the way you would want to find it when you return. Be a leader = teacher = disciplinarian on the way out just as on the way in. Celebrate the success. Then get over the hangover, get rested and get started home!

Post Trip

5

The American Alpine Club and the American Mountain Foundation ask each expedition they endorse or sponsor to provide a detailed post-expedition report. While these are excellent sources of information for later expeditions, there are flaws in the system. First, only Nepal requires expeditions be endorsed by their home climbing organization. As a result, the data is largely about Nepal. Few outside the AAC know about or even use the data bank.

Reports from any trip are a welcome addition to the data bank. Such reports create a valuable record of problems encountered. They are made available to anyone who requests them. They are not only helpful to future travelers, they often show patterns or consistent problems. For example, in the early 1990s, anecdotal evidence indicated that

Gentle Expeditions

many liaison officers were not even going near the mountain, much less fulfilling any useful role in monitoring impact or correcting unethical behavior. Many L.O.'s saw their assignment as not much more than an opportunity to supplement their government salary. Climbers knew the system was not working. Yet until this information was documented by specific expedition, it was of little use. After the consistent pattern had been reported by 20 or so expeditions, the AAC shared this information with the Ministries of Tourism in Nepal and Pakistan. Today, the L.O. system seems to be improving. Write down the situations encountered, the problems experienced, the solutions, and what did not work. Send this information to the AAC, the AMF, or both.

Whether this was a once-in-a-lifetime adventure, or whether thoughts now turn to the next trip, we tell others about our trips, often in slide shows. The content of these shows is predictable. There is the "getting through customs" epic, "the road was out and this is how we got through the landslide" epic, the "porters went on strike" epic, the crux of the climb and beautiful mountain scenery. All too often, the dark side of the story is left out of articles and slide shows. As a result, every team has to relearn for themselves what works. Consider showing audiences the environmental problems encountered and talking about how they were solved. This will increase awareness as to the fragility of remote

Post Trip

mountains. It will help those planning their own trips to consider, before they leave, how best to minimize their impact. Tell them about this book.

Find the right magazine and sell a story to help finance the next trip. Again, tell about the problems and how they were solved. Middendorf's article in *Climbing,* October-November 1993, takes the reader from the dream to the reality with good practical advice based on lessons learned. It reinforces the importance of a commitment from staff to help meet our goals. This is obviously tougher when the government representative is the problem. His article was sent to the President of the Pakistan Mountaineering Association; they are in the best position to change the behavior of L.O.'s. Those who are planning a trip to Pakistan can, based on his account, raise the issue of garbage and waste disposal when negotiating a permit.

In addition to sharing the dark side in articles, reports and "dirty picture shows," consider volunteering to teach others what was learned. The AAC, AMF, the Mountaineers in Seattle, and the Colorado Mountain Club, among others, are always looking for volunteers to help out on committees or specific projects. A good example is the work being done by AMF in the El Dorado Canyon climbing area near Boulder, Colorado. Look around, see what is going on near home, and get involved.

Where Do We Go From Here?

6

Forty years ago, Aldo Leopold lamented that modern equipment had robbed sportsmen of the "go-light, one-bullet-one-buck" ethic that had been a part of America's early history. He challenged us to give up craving the latest gadgets, observing that gadgets insulate their owners from the need to solve problems. Only after his reader had been hooked with the barb of guilt did he confide that he was a gadget fan himself. Admitting the line between acceptable and unacceptable gadgets is hard to identify, Leopold justified the inquiry by observing, "in these higher aspirations the important thing is not to achieve, but to strive."

The same problem exists today in differentiating between ethical and unethical behavior in the mountains. The line between style and ethics is not always bright; the answers are not easy. Yet it is worthwhile to strive towards answers, even at the risk we may not achieve universal agreement

Gentle Expeditions

A good test about crossing the ethical line is whether one's choice will either interfere with another's enjoyment of the mountains or will damage the mountains. If so, chances are the choice involves ethics rather than style. It is time to focus the inquiry, recognizing that try as we might, we will not always reach agreement on what is unethical. Certain behavior is clearly unjustified, should no longer be acceptable and as a result, is unethical.

This photograph, taken in the Annapurna Sanctuary in Nepal, shows unacceptable behavior. How can anyone justify spray painting graffiti on rocks in a protected wilderness area?

Annapurna Sanctuary, 1992.

Where Do We Go From Here?

Each of us who joins the inquiry should come away with a clearer view of what behavior is unacceptable. We should commit to avoiding this behavior ourselves. As Leopold pointed out, "voluntary adherence to an ethical code elevates the self-respect of the sportsman." As we have explored what is unethical, we have seen the advantages and disadvantages of various styles of behavior. Hopefully, this will encourage you to select from among acceptable styles of behavior one which will reduce the impact of mountain travel.

An expedition may choose to try a new route or to try one which is established and well known. This is a matter of style as either choice is acceptable. The choice of an established route may well give the team a greater likelihood of success in reaching their goal. While their choice may subject the team to criticism by others, it is theirs to make. Their behavior on the route they have chosen is another matter entirely. Spray painting graffiti or leaving piles of garbage would be unethical on any route.

As another example, a team may choose to climb with or without using fixed ropes. Again this is a question of style and either choice is acceptable. This example demonstrates that the choice one makes may create additional responsibilities. Failing to meet these responsibilities moves beyond style to an issue of ethics. The decision to use fixed ropes obligates the members of an expedition to remove these ropes when their climb is completed absent some unforseen emergency. Leaving fixed ropes on a route after a climb is completed may result in injury to others. Without question, it will spoil others' opportunity to "explore" the route just as the team putting in the first fixed ropes had the opportunity to explore. A similar responsibility arises when a team decides to use bottled oxygen. The choice is one of style. However, it is no longer ethical to leave empty oxygen bottles on a route after a climb is completed.

These examples should generate discussion, perhaps heated, and may generate dsagreement. If so, this book has been a success. Such discussions and even disagreement will clarify the difference between style and ethics. Mountain travelers, and more importantly the mountains we love, will benefit as a result.

ENFORCING ETHICAL BEHAVIOR

Climbers bristle at any attempt to police their behavior. Witness the controversy which has raged over bolting rock climbing routes. After all, part of the allure of climbing is the chance to escape from society's view of how one should behave. For many years, the question of

Where Do We Go From Here?

whether the members of an expedition had behaved unethically has been left to the members themselves. The sad reality is that far too many ignored their responsibility not to interfere with others' enjoyment of the mountains, and their responsibility to leave the mountains undamaged. As a result, the most remote and the most beautiful places on earth, from Everest to Antarctica, bear sad witness to the behavior of those who have been left to police themselves. How can people who profess to love the mountains behave in such a manner?

A line between acceptable choices of style and unacceptable (unethical) behavior does exist. Since that line can be identified, the question becomes what should happen to those who behave unethically. Should their behavior be ignored or should it be punished? A sign near Vail Pass, Colorado reads "$1,000 Fine For Littering Enforced." Aren't the Himalayas just as vulnerable to desecration as Vail Pass? Should unethical climbers be identified in climbing magazines? If so, would peer pressure begin to force behavior modification? Should they be denied access to the mountains? If so, for how long? It is time such questions were addressed.

Think what you would have done had you come upon the team spray painting their name in the Annapurna Sanctuary or a team departing basecamp leaving behind trash or materials identifying their expedition. One way to handle this, beyond ignoring it, would be to photograph what has been left. Send the photographs to the team and ask for an explanation. If no response is received, copies can be sent to the appropriate alpine club. If the team was American, the AAC would ask the team to justify their behavior. A record of such behavior would be considered in future requests for endorsement. Think about reporting what was observed to the entity issuing permits. Consider including photos in the story you tell or sell to one of the magazines.

Another level of inquiry arises when one witnesses unethical behavior. Examples run the gamut from others littering along the trail, to improperly disposing of human or food waste, to leaving fixed ropes or oxygen bottles, tents and other debris at a high camp. In such situations, one option is to point out to the individual or team how better to handle the same situation. For example, you are hauling out all litter, using porta-potties for human waste, have taken down your oxygen bottles, plan to take down fixed ropes, etc. Such conversation alone is often sufficient to jar a person's memory about the way they behave in their own country and remind them of their obligation as guests. If conversation does not produce the desired change

Where Do We Go From Here?

in behavior, pick it up yourself. Picking up litter in a camp still occupied by another team may shame them into modifying their behavior. There are obvious limits to the extent to which one could embark upon this type behavior without sacrificing one's own goals. One's entire trip might be consumed in cleaning up after other people.

Those are my thoughts on how to plan and participate in a gentle expedition, how we should behave in the mountains. These ideas work. If we don't all change how we behave in the mountains, future generations will never forgive us no matter how many videos or slides we show them of the great things we did in the mountains. The frightening thing is that there are pitiful few remaining unspoiled areas on earth. We must act now to preserve the pristine places and to restore the areas that have already suffered. Perhaps these ideas have caused you to pause and think about how you once behaved in the mountains. Think about the future.

Grafitti on rock, Paiju, Pakistan. CHARLEY MACE

APPENDICES

1. Resources

Alpine Club of Pakistan
509 Cashmere Rd RA Bazaar
Rawalpindi, Pakistan
Telephone: 011-562-918
Fax: 011-581-987

Amer. Consulate/
Chungdu, China
PSC 46 - Box 85
FPO AP 96521-0002
Fax: 011-86-285-83520

Amer. Himalayan Foundation
c/o Executive Director
909 Montgomery Street,
Suite 400
San Francisco, CA 94133
Phone: (415) 434-1111
Fax: (415) 434-3130

Annapurna Conservation-
Area Project
PO Box 3712, Babar Mahor
Kathmandu, Nepal
Phone: 977-1-220109
Fax: 977-1-226602

British Mt.ing Council
177Burton Rd./W. Didsbury,
Manchester M20 2BB/ U.K.
Phone: 011-0161-445-4747
Fax: 011-0161-445-4500

American Alpine Club
710 10th Street
Golden, Colorado 80401
Phone: (303) 384-0110 /
Fax: (303) 384-0111
E-Mail:
amalpine @ lx.netcom.com

American Embassy
New Delhi, India
Phone: 011-91-011-600-651
011-91-011-687-2028

Amer. Mountain Foundation
1520 Alamo Avenue
Colorado Springs, CO 80907
Phone: (719) 471-7736
Fax: (719) 577-4552
E-Mail:
mhesseamf @ aol.com

Bag Connection, Inc.
P.O. Box 817
Newburg, Oregon 97132
Phone: (503) 538-8180
Fax: (503) 538-0418.

China-Tibet Mt.ing Assoc.
No. 8 East Linkhor Road
Lhasa, Tibet, China
Phone: 011-0891-633-3720
Fax: 011-0891-633-6366

Gentle Expeditions

CIWEC Clinic
P.O. Box 1340
Kathmandu, Nepal
Phone: 011-977-1-410-983
Fax: 011-977-1-419-611

Everest Environmental Project
3730 Wind Dance Lane
Colorado Springs, CO 80906
Phone: (719) 578-9061
Fax: (719) 475-0858
E-mail : 102412.2564
@ compuserve.com
or liznichol @ aol.com

Hikers Against Doo
Box 271
Hampdon, MA 04444
Phone: (207) 223-4694

Indian Embassy
2107 Massachusetts Avenue, N.W.
Washington, D.C. 20008
Phone: (202) 939-7081
Fax: (202) 939-7027

Kathmandu Environmental
   Education Project
P.O. Box 4944
Tridevi Marg, Thamel
Kathmandu, Nepal
Phone: 011-977-1-418755
Fax: 011-977-1-411533
E-mail: keepukijw @ gn.apc.org

Colorado Mountain Club
710 10th Street, Suite 200
Golden, CO 80401
Phone: (303) 279-3080

Explorers Club
46 East 70th Street
New York, NY 10021
Phone: (212) 628-8383
Fax: (212) 288-4449

Himalayan Envir. Trust
82 Sainik Farms
New Delhi 110062/ India
Phone: 011-91-11-685-2593
Fax: 011-91-11-686-2374

Himalayan Mt.ing Institute
Darjeeling 734101 (W.B.) India
Phone: 011-0345-54083

Indian Mt.ng Foundation
Benito Juares Road
Anand Niketan
New Delhi 110021 India
Phone: 011-91-116-71211
Fax: 011-91-116- 883412

Ministry of Tourism
   and Civil Aviation
Kathmandu, Nepal
Phone: 011-977-121-1293
Fax: 011-977-122-7758

Appendix 1: Resources

The Mountain Institute
Main and Dogwood Streets
Franklin, WV 26807
Phone: (304) 358-2401
Fax: (304) 385-2400
E-mail: summit @ igc.apc.org

Nalge Company
75 Panorama Creek Dr.
P.O. Box 20365
Rochester, NY 14602-0365

Nepal Mountaineering Assoc.
Hattismar Naxal
P.O. Box 1435
Kathmandu, Nepal
Phone: 011-977-141-1525

Sagarmatha Pollution
    Control Project
PO Box 7660
Kathmandu, Nepal
Phone: 977-1- 410137
Fax: 977-1-410237

UIAA
Helvetiaplatz 4
Postfach
CH-3000 BERN 6
Switzerland
Phone: 011-4131-352-4624
Fax: 011-4131-352-8118

National Outdoor
 Leadership School
288 Main Street
Lander, Wyoming 82520
Phone: (307) 332-6973
Fax: (307) 332-3631

Nepal Embassy
2131 Leroy Place
Washington, D.C. 20008
Phone: (202) 667-4550

Real Goods Trading Co.
6 Mazzoni Street
Ukiah, California 95482
Phone: 1-800-762-7325
Fax: (707) 468-0301

Solar Box Cookers
1724 Eleventh St.
Sacramento, CA 95814
Phone: (916) 444-6616

Union Pan American
de Assoc. de Montanismo
Recalde 253 y AF. Avenue
Los Gasca, Quito
Ecuador
Fax: 011-593-244-0502

The Wisdom Light Group
(P. Ltd.)
P.O. Box 6191
Durbar Marg
Kathmandu, Nepal
Phone: 011-977-1-288-696
Fax: 011-977-1-288-696

Gentle Expeditions

2. UIAA Target Program For Waste Disposal

We tourists and mountaineers come from a society used to equipment, packaging and easy disposal and our habits produce waste that cannot be simply absorbed by nature. Tossed away, hidden and buried: our civilizational waste is out of place in the mountain landscape.

The UIAA-Program "Avoiding Trash and Waste Disposal" has been created to commit everyone involved in a trip to concentrate on a common goal, namely "clean mountains". In order to accomplish this, all must cooperate as partners:
- official associates in the countries visited,
- operators, organizers and expedition leaders,
- regional representatives in the countries visited
- mountain guides, expedition and tour leaders,
- producers and suppliers of equipment and provisions,
- and last not least, travellers themselves.

When planning a mountain trip, expedition, trek or individual tour, you should definitely observe two principles:
1) reduce the amount of trash produced as best possible;
2) dispose of the unavoidable waste by environmentally acceptable means.

In the following paragraphs, the UIAA has compiled a list of some of the most important rules of behaviour according to which the individual participants can critically review their travel preparations.

Appendix 2

A - <u>Information for Organizers of Treks and Expeditions, including Agencies.</u>

Your clients want to enjoy the beauty of the mountains, without trails and campsites lined with ugly trash and disfigured by dangerous waste. It is also in your interest to do everything possible to preserve the beauty of the mountains for your clients. We would like to help you to not leave any marks behind in the form of waste and trash on your treks.

To dispose of the waste in an environmentally safe way means:

1) bury decomposable trash;
2) burn burnable refuse;
3) remove problem waste out of region.

Planning and steps before starting a trek:

-Information and training for all staff members, office workers, guides, sirdars, cooks and kitchen teams as well as porters;

-Responsibility for using the program must be taken on by those in charge (guide, sirdar, one cook);

-Instructions for the cooks: no canned food. Every chance should be used to buy fresh fruit, vegetables and meat along the way

-Training for the kitchen teams to sort the trash according to decomposable trash, burnable trash and refuse to be removed (e.g., batteries, cartridges, kerosene drums, tin cases, plastic containers);

-Critical examination and selection of all materials taken along;

-Transportation of food in reusable containers only, including small ones that can be refilled after a

Gentle Expeditions

trek, such as for coffee, ketchup, curry sauce. Use of decomposable or burnable containers (paper, burlap, baskets);

-Organization ahead of time for the return transportation of the unavoidable waste (porters for packaging, pack animals).

Steps during a trek:
-Use of established campgrounds and firesites, make no open fires and economize with wood;
-Continual sorting of trash and its disposal or return transportation;
-Use of latrine-tents, proper coverage of the latrine site after dismantlement;
-It must be ensured that the lunch sites and tent grounds, base camps and high altitude are left absolutely clean. A daily final check by the person in charge is mandatory.

B - <u>Information for Mountain Guides, Expeditions and Tourleaders.</u>

You play a key role in the practical realization of the waste concept. Your experience and suggestions are included in the concept. You advise, inform and set good examples. You observe and influence behavior during tours and make decisions on locations (e.g., establishing campgrounds and sites). You supervise return transportation of problem waste.

C - <u>Information for Mountaineers, Trekkers and Individual Tourists.</u>

Appendix 2: UIAA Target Program

Travel lighter!

Take along only the most necessary personal gear. Try to do without some of the familiar goods of everyday life for a brief time. You will be less loaded and will be freer to experience the unknown.

And you will produce less waste. Do you really need:

- the walkman with cassettes and replacement batteries?
- the short wave radio and replacement batteries?
- the very large camera outfit and so many films?
- the overfilled washkit and so many medications?
- the large pack of moist towelettes, each individually sealed in foil?

Avoid Packaging Waste!

Pay careful attention that you take along equipment and supplies only in environmentally acceptable packaging and material. Aluminum foil, tin cans, plastic containers and glass bottles are trash that nature cannot digest. Whatever is not easily burnable or biodegradable should not be taken along.

Dispose at home.

Take on the problem waste that you could not (or did not want to) avoid back home again, in order to dispose of it in an environmentally suitable way. Batteries, aluminum foil, plastic, medications, etc., are products of our civilization. They do not belong in the mountain landscape, not even hidden or buried.

Gentle Expeditions

3. The Himalayan Tourist Code
(Published by the Britain Tourism Concern)

LIMIT DEFORESTATION - MAKE NO OPEN FIRES, and discourage others from doing so on your behalf. Where water is heated by scarce firewood, use as little as possible. When possible choose accommodations that use kerosene or fuel efficient wood stoves.

REMOVE LITTER - BURN or BURY paper products, and CARRY non-biodegradable rubbish out. Graffiti are permanent examples of environmental pollution.

KEEP LOCAL WATER CLEAN - avoid detergents and other pollutants in streams or springs. If no toilet facilities are available, make sure you are at least 30 meters from water sources, and bury or cover wastes.

PLANTS SHOULD BE LEFT TO FLOURISH IN THEIR NATURAL ENVIRONMENT - taking cuttings, seeds, and roots is illegal in many parts of the Himalaya.

HELP YOUR GUIDES and porters to follow conservation measures.

AS A GUEST, RESPECT LOCAL TRADITIONS, PROTECT LOCAL CULTURES, MAINTAIN LOCAL PRIDE.

WHEN TAKING PHOTOGRAPHS - ask permission; use restraint, and respect privacy.

RESPECT HOLY PLACES - preserve what you have come to see never touch or remove religious objects. Shoes should be removed when visiting temples.

Appendix 3

YOU WILL BE ACCEPTED AND WELCOMED IF YOU FOLLOW LOCAL CUSTOMS - use only your right hand for eating and greeting. At meal times do not share cutlery or cups, etc. It is polite to use both hands when giving or receiving gifts.

RESPECT FOR LOCAL ETIQUETTE EARNS YOU RESPECT - loose, light weight clothes are preferable to revealing shorts, skimpy tops and tight fitting "action wear." Hand holding or kissing in public are disliked by local people.

OBSERVE STANDARD FOOD AND BED CHARGES - but do not condone over charging. Remember when you're shopping, that the "bargains" you buy may only be possible because of the low income of others.

GIVING TO CHILDREN ENCOURAGES BEGGING - a donation to a project, health center, or school is a more constructive way to help.

VISITORS WHO VALUE LOCAL TRADITIONS - encourage local pride and maintain local cultures. Please help local people have a realistic view of life.

BE PATIENT, FRIENDLY and remember you are a guest.

**THE HIMALAYA MAY CHANGE YOU,
DO NOT CHANGE THEM!**

4. Suggested Packing List

Bio-degradable soap
Five gallon buckets with tight fitting lids
Funnels for pouring fuel
Inflatable globe
Insect repellant
Iodine solution
Lime
Malaria pills
<u>Medicine for Mountaineering</u>
Metal trays for pouring fuel
Mosquito coils
Mosquito nets
Phisohex
Pick
Pictures from home
Plastic or metal tubs for dishwashing
Responsible gifts for children (magic slates, writing pens and paper, tooth paste, vitamins, etc.)
Scrub brushes for hands and dishes
Shovel
Strainer
Surgical gloves
Syringes and needles
Toilet seat
Transfusion kit
Wands for marking toilet areas
Woven plastic or burlap bags

Appendix 5

5. Pre-Expedition Team Letter

Plans are shaping up for my next trip to Mount Everest. We have some money in the bank, endorsements from The American Alpine Club and The American Mountain Foundation and lots of enthusiasm. We are now ready to identify team members and begin fund-raising, environmental research and other preparations in earnest.

I would like to offer you a position as team member on the Expedition. Our plan is to leave the United States in July, 1992. We will do last minute shopping and coordination in Nepal and then travel overland to the Everest Base Camp in Tibet. We will spend approximately four weeks operating from a central location in or near basecamp.

Each team member must make a cash contribution to the Expedition of $1,000. This will be payable in the amount of $500 with your acceptance and $500 no later than January 1, 1992. Each must assist in pre-departure planning, preparation and fund-raising, and pay for their own air transportation (approximately $1,800) and personal equipment, to the extent it is not donated. We plan to hold several team meetings. If you cannot attend any meeting, you give your proxy to me to vote on all issues. The team may, by majority vote, remove any member before our departure for Tibet. Should that happen, your cash contribution would be refunded.

Each team member must release the Expedition, its sponsors and team members from any litigation arising out of your participation in any way in the project. I accept your offer to join the expedition and commit to minimum impact mountaineering. Enclosed is my check for $500.

If I am unable to attend team meetings, I appoint your proxy with full authority to vote on all issues.

(The letter closes with an agreement not to sue the expedition and a space for a signature.)

REFERENCES AND SUGGESTED READING

A Sand County Almanac, Leopold, Aldo, Ballantine Books, New York, 1991.

Annapurna. Herzog, Maurice. E.P. Dutton & Co., New York, 1953.

Beyond The Limits; A Woman's Triumph on Everest. Allison, Stacey. Doubleday, New York, 1996.

Conservation is the Ethic of the Future, King Mahendra Trust for Nature Conservation. (Available: P.O. Box 3712, Kathmandu, Phone: 011-977-526-571 / Fax:977-526-570.)

Everest. Unsworth, Walt. Grafton Books, 1991.

Everest; The Best Writing and Pictures From Seventy Years of Human Endeavor. Gillman, Peter (editor). Little, Brown and Co., Boston, 1993.

Everest, The Testing Place. West, Dr. John B. McGraw-Hill Book Co., New York, 1985.

Everest, A Sound History 1922-1983. Listen for Pleasure Ltd. (Available: 111 Martin Ross Avenue, Downsview, Ontario, Canada M3J 2M1.)

How To Shit In The Woods. Meyer, Kathleen. Ten Speed Press, Berkeley, 1994.

If Mountains Die. Nichols, John. Alfred A. Knoff, New York, 1987.

K-2: The Story of the Savage Mountain. Curran, Jim. The Mountaineers Books, Seattle, 1995.

Let the Mountains Talk, Let the Rivers Run. Brower, David. Harper Collins West, New York, 1995.

References/Suggested Reading

Low-Impact Recreational Practices for Wilderness and Backcountry. Cole, David N. U.S. Department of Agriculture, Forest Service, General Technical Report INT-265, 1989. (Available: Intermountain Research Station, 324 25th Street, Ogden, UT 84401.)

Medicine for Mountaineering. Wilkerson, James A., M.D. The Mountaineers Books, Seattle, 1993.

Mountain Sickness. Hackett, Dr. Peter H. The American Alpine Club, Golden, CO, 1996.

NOLS Wilderness Mountaineering. Powers, Phil. Stackpole Books, Mechanicsburg, PA, 1993.

Procedures for Mountaineering Expeditions in Tibet. China-Tibet Mountaineer Association. (Available: No. 8 East Linkhor Road, Lhasa, Tibet, China, Phone: 011-0891-633-3720 / Fax: 011-0891-633-6366.)

Sherpas: Reflections on Change in Himalayan Nepal.. Fisher, James F. University of California Press, Berkley, 1990.

Soft Paths. Hampton, Bruce and David Cole. Stackpole Books, Mechanicsburg, PA, 1988.

The Climber's Handbook, Sierra Club Books, San Francisco, 1987. (An excellent book with sections on rock, ice and alpine climbing as well as expeditions.)

The Conquest of Everest. Hunt, Sir John. E.P. Dutton & Co., New York, 1954.

Trekking Gently in the Himalaya. Lama, Wendy Brewer. Sagarmatha Pollution Control Project, 1992. (Available: Environmental Education Project, P.O. Box 224, Kathmandu, Nepal; send author $1.)

Gentle Expeditions

Trekking in Tibet. McCue, Gary. The Mountaineers Books, Seattle, 1991.

Walking Softly In The Wilderness. Hart, John. Little, Brown & Co., Boston, 1982.

Wilderness Ethics. Waterman, Laura and Guy. Countryman Press, Woodstock, VT, 1993.

About the Author

Bob McConnell serves on the Board of Directors of the American Alpine Club. He cochairs its Conservation Committee, is cofounder and director of the Everest Environmental Project, and is a technical advisor to the Amereican Mountain Foundation. The author led the 1990 and 1992 Everest Environmental Expeditions, and has participated in five expeditions to Nepal, Tibet, and India.

NOTES

NOTES

NOTES

NOTES

NOTES

NOTES

NOTES

NOTES

NOTES